The Zen Book
of
Weekly Planning
for a
Fulfilling Life

Activinotes

Activinotes

DAILY JOURNALS, PLANNERS, NOTEBOOKS AND OTHER BLANK BOOKS

Weekly Planner

Weekly Planner

MONDAY	TUESDAY	WEDNESDAY

THURSDAY	FRIDAY	SATURDAY

SUNDAY

When you're busy creating your own fulfillment,
You won't feel the need to seek it from others.

Weekly Planner

To Do	Reminder	To Buy

Weekly Planner

MONDAY	TUESDAY	WEDNESDAY

THURSDAY	FRIDAY	SATURDAY

SUNDAY

When you're busy creating your own fulfillment,
You won't feel the need to seek it from others.

Weekly Planner

To Do	Reminder	To Buy

☯ Weekly Planner ☯

MONDAY	TUESDAY	WEDNESDAY

THURSDAY	FRIDAY	SATURDAY

SUNDAY

When you're busy creating your own fulfillment,
You won't feel the need to seek it from others.

Weekly Planner

To Do	Reminder	To Buy

☯ Weekly Planner ☯

MONDAY	TUESDAY	WEDNESDAY

THURSDAY	FRIDAY	SATURDAY

SUNDAY

When you're busy creating your own fulfillment,
You won't feel the need to seek it from others.

☯ Weekly Planner ☯

To Do	Reminder	To Buy

Weekly Planner

MONDAY	TUESDAY	WEDNESDAY

THURSDAY	FRIDAY	SATURDAY

SUNDAY

When you're busy creating your own fulfillment,
You won't feel the need to seek it from others.

Weekly Planner

To Do	Reminder	To Buy

Weekly Planner

MONDAY	TUESDAY	WEDNESDAY

THURSDAY	FRIDAY	SATURDAY

SUNDAY

When you're busy creating your own fulfillment,
You won't feel the need to seek it from others.

Weekly Planner

To Do	Reminder	To Buy

Weekly Planner

MONDAY	TUESDAY	WEDNESDAY

THURSDAY	FRIDAY	SATURDAY

SUNDAY

When you're busy creating your own fulfillment,
You won't feel the need to seek it from others.

Weekly Planner

To Do

Reminder

To Buy

Weekly Planner

MONDAY	TUESDAY	WEDNESDAY

THURSDAY	FRIDAY	SATURDAY

SUNDAY

When you're busy creating your own fulfillment,
You won't feel the need to seek it from others.

Weekly Planner

To Do	Reminder	To Buy

Weekly Planner

MONDAY	TUESDAY	WEDNESDAY

THURSDAY	FRIDAY	SATURDAY

SUNDAY

When you're busy creating your own fulfillment,
You won't feel the need to seek it from others.

Weekly Planner

To Do	Reminder	To Buy

Weekly Planner

MONDAY	TUESDAY	WEDNESDAY

THURSDAY	FRIDAY	SATURDAY

SUNDAY

When you're busy creating your own fulfillment,
You won't feel the need to seek it from others.

Weekly Planner

To Do

Reminder

To Buy

Weekly Planner

MONDAY	TUESDAY	WEDNESDAY

THURSDAY	FRIDAY	SATURDAY

SUNDAY

When you're busy creating your own fulfillment,
You won't feel the need to seek it from others.

Weekly Planner

To Do

Reminder

To Buy

☯ Weekly Planner ☯

MONDAY	TUESDAY	WEDNESDAY

THURSDAY	FRIDAY	SATURDAY

SUNDAY

When you're busy creating your own fulfillment,
You won't feel the need to seek it from others.

Weekly Planner

To Do	Reminder	To Buy

Weekly Planner

MONDAY	TUESDAY	WEDNESDAY

THURSDAY	FRIDAY	SATURDAY

SUNDAY

When you're busy creating your own fulfillment,
You won't feel the need to seek it from others.

Weekly Planner

To Do	Reminder	To Buy

Weekly Planner

MONDAY	TUESDAY	WEDNESDAY

THURSDAY	FRIDAY	SATURDAY

SUNDAY

When you're busy creating your own fulfillment,
You won't feel the need to seek it from others.

Weekly Planner

To Do	Reminder	To Buy

Weekly Planner

MONDAY	TUESDAY	WEDNESDAY

THURSDAY	FRIDAY	SATURDAY

SUNDAY

When you're busy creating your own fulfillment,
You won't feel the need to seek it from others.

Weekly Planner

To Do	Reminder	To Buy

Weekly Planner

MONDAY	TUESDAY	WEDNESDAY

THURSDAY	FRIDAY	SATURDAY

SUNDAY

When you're busy creating your own fulfillment,
You won't feel the need to seek it from others.

Weekly Planner

To Do

Reminder

To Buy

Weekly Planner

MONDAY	TUESDAY	WEDNESDAY

THURSDAY	FRIDAY	SATURDAY

SUNDAY

When you're busy creating your own fulfillment,
You won't feel the need to seek it from others.

Weekly Planner

To Do	Reminder	To Buy

☯ Weekly Planner ☯

MONDAY	TUESDAY	WEDNESDAY

THURSDAY	FRIDAY	SATURDAY

SUNDAY

When you're busy creating your own fulfillment,
You won't feel the need to seek it from others.

Weekly Planner

To Do	Reminder	To Buy

Weekly Planner

MONDAY	TUESDAY	WEDNESDAY

THURSDAY	FRIDAY	SATURDAY

SUNDAY

When you're busy creating your own fulfillment,
You won't feel the need to seek it from others.

Weekly Planner

To Do	Reminder	To Buy

Weekly Planner

MONDAY	TUESDAY	WEDNESDAY

THURSDAY	FRIDAY	SATURDAY

SUNDAY

When you're busy creating your own fulfillment,
You won't feel the need to seek it from others.

Weekly Planner

To Do	Reminder	To Buy

Weekly Planner

MONDAY	TUESDAY	WEDNESDAY

THURSDAY	FRIDAY	SATURDAY

SUNDAY

When you're busy creating your own fulfillment,
You won't feel the need to seek it from others.

Weekly Planner

To Do	Reminder	To Buy

Weekly Planner

MONDAY	TUESDAY	WEDNESDAY

THURSDAY	FRIDAY	SATURDAY

SUNDAY

When you're busy creating your own fulfillment,
You won't feel the need to seek it from others.

Weekly Planner

To Do

Reminder

To Buy

Weekly Planner

MONDAY	TUESDAY	WEDNESDAY

THURSDAY	FRIDAY	SATURDAY

SUNDAY

When you're busy creating your own fulfillment,
You won't feel the need to seek it from others.

Weekly Planner

To Do	Reminder	To Buy

☯ Weekly Planner ☯

MONDAY	TUESDAY	WEDNESDAY

THURSDAY	FRIDAY	SATURDAY

SUNDAY

When you're busy creating your own fulfillment,
You won't feel the need to seek it from others.

Weekly Planner

To Do	Reminder	To Buy

Weekly Planner

MONDAY	TUESDAY	WEDNESDAY

THURSDAY	FRIDAY	SATURDAY

SUNDAY

When you're busy creating your own fulfillment,
You won't feel the need to seek it from others.

Weekly Planner

To Do

Reminder

To Buy

Weekly Planner

MONDAY	TUESDAY	WEDNESDAY

THURSDAY	FRIDAY	SATURDAY

SUNDAY

When you're busy creating your own fulfillment,
You won't feel the need to seek it from others.

Weekly Planner

To Do	Reminder	To Buy

Weekly Planner

MONDAY	TUESDAY	WEDNESDAY

THURSDAY	FRIDAY	SATURDAY

SUNDAY

When you're busy creating your own fulfillment,
You won't feel the need to seek it from others.

Weekly Planner

To Do	Reminder	To Buy

Weekly Planner

MONDAY	TUESDAY	WEDNESDAY

THURSDAY	FRIDAY	SATURDAY

SUNDAY

When you're busy creating your own fulfillment,
You won't feel the need to seek it from others.

Weekly Planner

To Do	Reminder	To Buy

Weekly Planner

MONDAY	TUESDAY	WEDNESDAY

THURSDAY	FRIDAY	SATURDAY

SUNDAY

When you're busy creating your own fulfillment,
You won't feel the need to seek it from others.

Weekly Planner

To Do

Reminder

To Buy

Weekly Planner

MONDAY	TUESDAY	WEDNESDAY

THURSDAY	FRIDAY	SATURDAY

SUNDAY

When you're busy creating your own fulfillment,
You won't feel the need to seek it from others.

Weekly Planner

To Do	Reminder	To Buy

Weekly Planner

MONDAY	TUESDAY	WEDNESDAY

THURSDAY	FRIDAY	SATURDAY

SUNDAY

When you're busy creating your own fulfillment,
You won't feel the need to seek it from others.

Weekly Planner

To Do	Reminder	To Buy

Weekly Planner

MONDAY	TUESDAY	WEDNESDAY

THURSDAY	FRIDAY	SATURDAY

SUNDAY

When you're busy creating your own fulfillment,
You won't feel the need to seek it from others.

Weekly Planner

To Do	Reminder	To Buy

Weekly Planner

MONDAY	TUESDAY	WEDNESDAY

THURSDAY	FRIDAY	SATURDAY

SUNDAY

When you're busy creating your own fulfillment,
You won't feel the need to seek it from others.

Weekly Planner

To Do

Reminder

To Buy

Weekly Planner

MONDAY	TUESDAY	WEDNESDAY

THURSDAY	FRIDAY	SATURDAY

SUNDAY

When you're busy creating your own fulfillment,
You won't feel the need to seek it from others.

Weekly Planner

To Do	Reminder	To Buy

Weekly Planner

MONDAY	TUESDAY	WEDNESDAY

THURSDAY	FRIDAY	SATURDAY

SUNDAY

When you're busy creating your own fulfillment,
You won't feel the need to seek it from others.

Weekly Planner

To Do	Reminder	To Buy

Weekly Planner

MONDAY	TUESDAY	WEDNESDAY

THURSDAY	FRIDAY	SATURDAY

SUNDAY

When you're busy creating your own fulfillment,
You won't feel the need to seek it from others.

Weekly Planner

To Do	Reminder	To Buy

Weekly Planner

MONDAY	TUESDAY	WEDNESDAY

THURSDAY	FRIDAY	SATURDAY

SUNDAY

When you're busy creating your own fulfillment,
You won't feel the need to seek it from others.

Weekly Planner

To Do

Reminder

To Buy

☯ Weekly Planner ☯

MONDAY	TUESDAY	WEDNESDAY

THURSDAY	FRIDAY	SATURDAY

SUNDAY

When you're busy creating your own fulfillment,
You won't feel the need to seek it from others.

Weekly Planner

To Do	Reminder	To Buy

☯ Weekly Planner ☯

MONDAY	TUESDAY	WEDNESDAY

THURSDAY	FRIDAY	SATURDAY

SUNDAY

When you're busy creating your own fulfillment,
You won't feel the need to seek it from others.

Weekly Planner

To Do	Reminder	To Buy

☯ Weekly Planner ☯

MONDAY	TUESDAY	WEDNESDAY

THURSDAY	FRIDAY	SATURDAY

SUNDAY

When you're busy creating your own fulfillment,
You won't feel the need to seek it from others.

Weekly Planner

To Do	Reminder	To Buy

Weekly Planner

MONDAY	TUESDAY	WEDNESDAY

THURSDAY	FRIDAY	SATURDAY

SUNDAY

When you're busy creating your own fulfillment,
You won't feel the need to seek it from others.

Weekly Planner

To Do	Reminder	To Buy

Weekly Planner

MONDAY	TUESDAY	WEDNESDAY

THURSDAY	FRIDAY	SATURDAY

SUNDAY

When you're busy creating your own fulfillment,
You won't feel the need to seek it from others.

Weekly Planner

To Do	Reminder	To Buy

Weekly Planner

MONDAY	TUESDAY	WEDNESDAY

THURSDAY	FRIDAY	SATURDAY

SUNDAY

When you're busy creating your own fulfillment,
You won't feel the need to seek it from others.

Weekly Planner

To Do	Reminder	To Buy

☯ Weekly Planner ☯

MONDAY	TUESDAY	WEDNESDAY

THURSDAY	FRIDAY	SATURDAY

SUNDAY

When you're busy creating your own fulfillment,
You won't feel the need to seek it from others.

Weekly Planner

To Do	Reminder	To Buy

Weekly Planner

MONDAY	TUESDAY	WEDNESDAY

THURSDAY	FRIDAY	SATURDAY

SUNDAY

When you're busy creating your own fulfillment,
You won't feel the need to seek it from others.

Weekly Planner

To Do

Reminder

To Buy

Weekly Planner

MONDAY	TUESDAY	WEDNESDAY

THURSDAY	FRIDAY	SATURDAY

SUNDAY

When you're busy creating your own fulfillment,
You won't feel the need to seek it from others.

Weekly Planner

To Do	Reminder	To Buy

☯ Weekly Planner ☯

MONDAY	TUESDAY	WEDNESDAY

THURSDAY	FRIDAY	SATURDAY

SUNDAY

When you're busy creating your own fulfillment,
You won't feel the need to seek it from others.

Weekly Planner

To Do	Reminder	To Buy

Weekly Planner

MONDAY	TUESDAY	WEDNESDAY

THURSDAY	FRIDAY	SATURDAY

SUNDAY

When you're busy creating your own fulfillment,
You won't feel the need to seek it from others.

Weekly Planner

To Do	Reminder	To Buy

Weekly Planner

MONDAY	TUESDAY	WEDNESDAY

THURSDAY	FRIDAY	SATURDAY

SUNDAY

When you're busy creating your own fulfillment,
You won't feel the need to seek it from others.

Weekly Planner

To Do	Reminder	To Buy

☯ Weekly Planner ☯

MONDAY	TUESDAY	WEDNESDAY

THURSDAY	FRIDAY	SATURDAY

SUNDAY

When you're busy creating your own fulfillment,
You won't feel the need to seek it from others.

Weekly Planner

To Do

Reminder

To Buy

Weekly Planner

Notes

www.ingramcontent.com/pod-product-compliance
Lightning Source LLC
Chambersburg PA
CBHW081338090426
42737CB00017B/3196